Cover design by 120 Design Studio

http://120designstudio.com

There is no greater agony than bearing an untold story inside you.

— Maya Angelou

Writing Is Essential

USE THE SKILLS YOU'VE GOT TO GET THE JOB DONE

UNITED
BLACK
WRITERS
ASSOCIATION

For more information contact:
United Black Writers Association, Inc.
PO Box 1449
Hyattsville, MD 20785

ByAnyInkNecessary.org

Dedicated to our parents:
Wouldn't be where we are without them.

Words of Recommendation

"This work has to be done. Our history is in the social landscape. We have to write about it," says Angela Puryear-McDuffie, who collected tales from people in her Washington, D.C. neighborhood in order to craft a narrative history of the community. Though focused specifically on African American writers, any reader dreaming about becoming an author will find support here. Everyone has a story, and anyone can become an author, according to this encouraging and worthy book."   — *Kirkus Reviews*

"Inspiring and full of hope for writers everywhere. Most important of all, this book gives us the sense of our need for diversity in stories and the writers that give us those stories. Writing is Essential is both a true statement and a step toward a great future in storytelling."
                                    — *Kathy Carberry, Goodreads Reviewer*

"This was a quick and fascinating read that I highly recommend for both writers and people eager to vividly see life from several nuanced perspectives."   — *Em, Goodreads Reviewer*

"These are the types of conversations that keep me writing even when it seems like sometimes the words escape me."
                                    — *Dora Okeyo, Goodreads Reviewer*

"This book featured several interviews with POC (people of color) authors … and many were quite honest about their writing process and inspiration. Good read if you have writer's block and need a pick-me-up."
                                    — *Suzanne Bhagan, Goodreads Reviewer*

"A great read for any aspiring writer. The interviews are insightful and offers great inspiration for those who may be struggling with believing in themselves and their dreams."   — *Suzette, Goodreads Reviewer*

"First, I loved the interview setup of this book. It was conversational and very inviting. Second, I appreciated the content of the book. I believe it's important to hear people's stories — this book is a study in the events that shape writers."   — *DrJReads.blogspot.com*

Runnin' on empty,
there was nothin' left in me
but doubt;
I picked up a pen
and I wrote my way out.

— Nas

Table of Contents

One of the many things I have always loved about writing (not to be confused with publishing) is that all you need is your imagination. It doesn't matter who you are, you can write.

— Roxane Gay

Introduction

Peace and Blessings to you!

In 2018, I set out on an incredible journey to interview writers from various walks of life. This was purely an assignment from the Creator, as I am a very introverted person, being more comfortable behind the camera and not in front of it.

Most of the interviews took place in the ELife Media Group recording studio on the "By Any Ink Necessary" show. Then I began traveling, "Spilling Ink," to cities throughout the US. I'm glad to have fulfilled the Creator's mission, as each writer provided valuable information about writing, publishing, or being an entrepreneur. I am grateful for the contributors, the cover designer Marshall Fox, the editors Rebecca Bishophall and Michelle Denenkamp, and Al-Qamar Malik for her continuous positivity. Without my tribe this project would not have been possible.

In this collection of edited interviews, there's a uniqueness in each dialogue; yet the same resounding message... just write!

Sincerely,
Judine Slaughter
Executive Director,
United Black Writers Association, Inc.

ByAnyInkNecessary.org

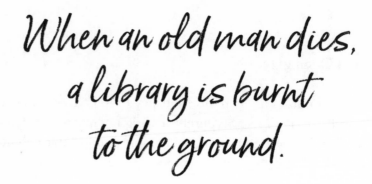

When an old man dies,
a library is burnt
to the ground.

— African Proverb

Angela Puryear-McDuffie

Tell us about yourself.

Angela: The name given to me at birth was Angela Beatrice Puryear. Beatrice, my mother's first name, was her inheritance to me. I was raised in Southeast Washington, DC, at the bottom of Alabama Avenue, an area we call Simple City. I'm exceptionally proud of where I'm from, and a lot of what I do as it relates to writing comes from Southeast DC's rich history. The stories and the narratives of my people are important to me. Those people who are important in my life, I want their stories told by people who loved them, told by the people who know them. I believe a lot of Simple City's history is in obscurity, because it's been told as a social commentary by onlookers, people who can't possibly know what it is they're looking at.

I recently started a cake business by the name of Beloveds Cakes, Treats & Savory. The name Beloveds comes from my grandmother, Mrs. Mildred Bynum, who taught me how to bake cakes, because of her own inability in her later years to use her hands from rheumatoid arthritis. I became her hands. She shared with me how to cook and how to bake cakes. After she passed away in October 2014, suddenly I started baking cakes all the time. I would be in the kitchen baking cakes when my friends and family would come to visit. Eventually my friends convinced me to sell the cakes. They didn't want me to tell them that I couldn't sell them a cake, because I was too busy, or I couldn't make a cake for them when they all wanted cakes. And they said, "You can't make everybody a cake for free; you have to charge us." That's when I started selling the cakes.

When my grandmother taught me how to cook, she did a great job. She wasn't just teaching me how to cook. She shared with me how to care for others, and now I bake in honor of her legacy. My grandmother also shared her stories with me, and I had the divine inspiration to record those stories. From listening to my grandmother's narratives and then starting the cake business, I realized baking and sharing stories was a major purpose for my life. I've started collecting narratives of individuals who have had some connection with the social landscape of Alabama Avenue in Southeast Washington, DC, and I'm now in the process of documenting the information. I'm writing these narratives to speak up for myself and contribute to the historical narratives of my African American community, and to help us begin to speak for ourselves.

This work has to be done. Our history is in the social landscape. We have to write about it. You know what happens if somebody else is writing your history? Any comment they made about you becomes your entire history, because you didn't write anything about yourself. Even in John 8:6, Christ physically wrote in the sand with his finger. If we don't write our own history, others might write all kinds of things concerning us and it can be skewed.

I would just advise everyone, if you have somebody in your family who is older, you should start recording their stories. At the advice of Deontae Smith, currently Deacon-in-Training at The New

Macedonia Baptist Church and my Brother in Christ, he generously helped me formulate the first plans for my business. I'm going to start putting the historical narratives on my cake boxes. When you buy a cake, you'll also get a piece of history from the street where you have bought your cake. I am not about making money, but rather building our community.

In the summer of 2018, my birth son, Benjamin Abdelrahman, a Minister at The New Macedonia Baptist Church, suggested I have an event twice a month called Single Serving Sundays. Beloveds Cakes, Treats & Savory partners with other entrepreneurs, individuals who are local, positive, and have a service or product to share with others. Beloveds Cakes, Treats & Savory participates by selling slices of cake with my business partner and son in the faith, Ashley Harris, who sells the treats and savory items, such as quiche, cheesecake and banana pudding. It can be a lot of food passing hands on any Single Serving Sunday. It's not just about me selling cakes, but it really is about community.

As I mentioned earlier, the name Beloveds comes from my grand-mother. Whenever the family came together, she would admonish us to stay united to understand the importance of community, the importance of loving one another. When she really got into it, I don't know what she was thinking about, maybe there was a rift in the family, and maybe some people weren't getting along. I think from her perspective, she would start admonishing us to unify and the tears would stream down her face, and she would say, "Beloveds, you've got to love one another, like Christ loved the church." At the end of the day you might think you have this or that, but family is always going to be family.

I'm grateful for my grandmother because my parents had prob-lems; they had issues that kept them from being good parents. But my grandparents were the backbone for every single branch of our family. My grandmother knew everything, because she sought it out.

Since she's passed, I realize through her absence what I no longer have because of the person she was. When she knew two people weren't getting along, she got on that phone and called to say, "I'm just calling to check you out." If she was "checking you out," by the time you finished talking to her, she knew your story; she'd figured it out. In truth, Grandma brought and kept our family together.

Judine: Omar Tyree helped Marion Barry, Jr. to write his story before he passed. Mr. Barry was able to tell the story about his family and four terms as Washington, DC's mayor, in his way. That's very important.

Angela: It's vital. We think of the material things we want to leave to our children. However, we need to think about leaving our ancestor's history to the younger generation. Where are they going to get the information, the history? My grandmother would ask me, "Who are you? You can talk from where you're from. You don't have to try to be like anybody else. You be yourself." She also gave me stories and a narrative that I could look back on that were positive. Everybody belongs to a family, even if they are not your biological family.

For example, my son is mentoring two young men in our neighborhood and teaching them how to write their narratives. They wanted to learn how to rap, and he said, "I will not teach you how to rap when every other word is a curse word. Why would I teach you how to spew what is killing you, destroying you?" Those young boys are now writing poetry, which doesn't have any curse words. One young man, when he first started writing, it was full of curse words and it was about committing suicide. That's what he knew.

I've also encouraged these young men by giving them a project to write the story of the land near Fort Dupont Park on Alabama Avenue. It took four tries. Finally, I got two run-on sentences; oh, they thought it was paragraphs! But I gave them a piece of cake anyway. First, it wasn't plagiarized and second, they tried to put their own words on paper the best way they knew. And that's where you start. These boys belong to a community, no matter what deep things may be going on in their families, which might speak to them to say, "You don't belong to anything." That's just not true. You belong to a community and you have value. For some the value of their today is based on them understanding that tomorrow people are going to look back to know everything about you. Writing can give them that gift, if we show them how to share their stories.

You have to write today, because future generations will be looking for your story. I have researched my family's genealogy, especially using the census. I've found my great-great-great-great-grandparents. I've traced my family back to 1835 and I think, "Did they know I was going to be looking for them?" We're connected. I think about all the records that are in churches, all the records that are in cemeteries. Writing about our ancestors, that's what you leave to future generations.

Judine: Whether you've written your story on paper, or written it on someone else's soul, you're still writing. Every day is a new chapter or a new story in your life.

Angela: That's why your life should be honest. You should live with integrity. It's just like trying to change history. You can't change history, because once the day is gone, you're on to another. You can't do anything about it. If you look at the landscape, if you look at where people live, if you look at what people did in that space, that's going to tell you the history of the people. That's the real history. We're connected on Alabama Avenue. We're connected, vitally connected, to America's Civil War. We're surrounded by forts.

Judine: Yes, in DC we are surrounded by forts. There's Fort Davis Park, next to Fort Dupont Park, and many others throughout the city. Fort Stevens, built for the American Civil War battle in 1864, has a stone memorial and cannons, which are maintained by the National Park Service.

Angela: When those young men were across the street writing, they were literally walking on the land a Civil War soldier walked on. They were inside the territory where someone fought in the Civil War. Then I asked, "What do you do in the landscape?" It's about preserving and conserving our history. My goal is to write several books about DC's rich history. When you understand who you are, from the perspective of where you are, then your purpose can be birthed. You are capable of doing what you were born to do.

Judine: You don't want the youth to listen to the story of DC painted by the media in the evening news. They have a different story and that's what they need to tell. They need your encouragement not to listen to what other people are saying could be their story. They have to realize that they are the writer of their own story.

Where has your writing taken you?

Angela: When I was a student at Trinity University, I double majored in history and political science. I won a scholarship to study abroad in Cyprus after writing a paper for a U.S. Intelligence course. The paper was a comparative analysis of democracy and its articulation between an ethnically diverse and a homogenous African culture post colonialism. Once in Cyprus, I completed an internship with the Cultural Heritage Center where I selected five churches to study that had sedimentary history back to the Pliocene period. I found documentation of relics and shards discovered that traced history through the Crusades into the Modern and post Modern era. From this research, I presented a report as a part of the final program for the class entitled "Historic Churches of Old Nicosia: Patterns in Society: The Power of Place Making." Because of the scholarship, I had the opportunity to live in Cyprus for a semester. I left the United States in August 2007 and returned in December that same year. I traveled to Italy, Greece, and spent Christmas in Dorset, England surrounded by rivers that enter the English Channel. From writing a paper, I was able to win this great opportunity to travel abroad, and experience a beautiful, magical time with other cultures.

I credit everything that I am to God's grace, because it could have been another way. Absolutely my life started out in one direction, but God steered it in a different direction. He made my life what it is today; it pours out of me into the community, into areas where Single Serving Sundays is an open platform for other businesses.

Who wrote on your soul to change your path?

Angela: My grandmother definitely wrote on my soul. She said, "I'm not going to let you have that miserable life that you're trying to have. You're trying to have that miserable life, but I am not going to let you have it." I came back to her for everything. No matter what was happening in my life, no matter where I was located, no matter what kind of lifestyle I was living, I always found my way back to my grandmother.

A lot of times we're in public, and we see young mothers snatching their kids, and yelling at their kids. We develop a disdain from what we see when in fact they need compassion. The disdain is why they're acting the way that they do. They have been dealing with that disdain for their children and a disdain even for themselves. I'm currently working with a few young adult mothers to write a different story on their souls.

Judine: The disdain is a form of genocide, because they are only acting the way their parents have acted, and their parents before. Just as there were people in your life writing on your soul to make sure that you went down a different path, I'm glad you are passing the torch by changing lives and learned patterns.

Can an entrepreneur survive on one stream of income?

Angela: Oh no, I couldn't. I have a full-time job, and then when I come home, I spend anywhere from seven to 13 hours during the week baking cakes, depending on how many cakes I have to bake. I step out on faith every day.

How else do you use writing in your lifestyle?

Angela: My phone has become my main writing instrument. It used to be strips or pieces of paper that I would grab and write anything. But now I use the notes app on my phone. I have lists that I absolutely have to keep, and the biggest thing that I'm writing now is my budget and my business plan. You cannot run an effective business without writing.

In 2018, I enrolled in the culinary school at Prince George's Community College. I've got to figure out how to hone my craft.

Judine: Everyone should always be trying to upgrade their skills. Even though you think might know everything there is to know about baking cakes with your grandmother's knowledge, you are still now going back to learn more. You want to learn what you can to bake even better cakes.

Angela: Right. For example, this interview is in a vegan restaurant. I would love to bake a super moist, delicious vegan cake. But I can't even begin to know where to start. And I also realize I'm entering an industry I know absolutely nothing about. There are people in this industry who have been to culinary school, and I want to know what they know.

What lessons have you learned as an entrepreneur?

Angela: I've learned that passion will take you further than anything else. You have to do what you want to do. You can tell somebody all day long, "Oh, I'm so sorry I didn't do that; I really wanted to." Whatever you did instead, that's what you really wanted to do. Even if it was just sleeping, whatever it is you want to do, you will do it. I always wanted to get my degree, and I attended Trinity University, but I had a passion for history. I took everything I could take in history and then I needed six credits to graduate and I literally could not find anything that I really wanted to take. But everybody told me, "Take anything. All you need are six credits to graduate." And I absolutely could not do it. I am now in culinary school and these are the six credits that I'll use to obtain my history degree.

Judine: If you had received your degree earlier in life, you might not have thought to go to culinary school. That's wonderful how it came back around. It all happened at the right time. It had to happen this way.

If you could tell your younger self anything about writing, what would you tell her?

Angela: Keep doing it. Keep doing it. That's your voice. Write it. When I was a kid, I wrote poetry, because I was hurting so badly from circumstances and situations. I've got volumes and volumes of poetry that's pretty darn good. I would tell my younger self that it's going to be okay. I was very conflicted about not having things that other people had, not being what I thought I saw other people being who were my age. Now I'm older, and I know it's okay. It's going to be all right.

What advice do you have for aspiring entrepreneurs?

Angela: Spend as much time as possible learning about yourself and your passions; what it is that you really want to do. Hone your craft. I had to go to college to learn I had a passion for history. I took a course at Trinity University, called Social Landscapes in U.S. Culture, taught by Sister Mary Hayes. I read a book by Dolores Hayden, titled *The Power of Place: Urban Landscapes as Public History.* She introduced me to looking at history using the tools of "shared memory and place-specific memory" in order to identify and analyze history from the perspective of the social landscape as opposed to national monuments built to celebrate and honor war heroes and conflict. When you see all of these conflicts about the confederate flag, it's a shared memory conflict. The flag is a conflict; that is very place-specific memory based on cultural experience. That flag means denied access to me; however, it's not that to other American people. It's similar to somebody telling me not to call the area I'm from on Alabama Avenue "Simple City." I tell them, "You're not from Simple City, therefore you don't know what I mean when I say Simple City." Simple City means so much more to me than you know, based on a very place-specific memory.

Judine: For some, Simple City might sound like a derogatory term, but for you it's an affectionate term because that's where you grew up. That's your place-specific memory of the section in DC where you live.

Angela: Absolutely. That belongs to me, and I'm not going to allow you to take that from me. For example, when I see the conflict between African Americans and White America over monuments, I think to myself, "It's about time we had this dialogue because you don't see many African American statues in public spaces. The civil war monuments have a place; put them in a museum."

Judine: What country allows the defeated nation to fly their flag? Nowhere is the defeated nation allowed to fly their flag. The confederacy didn't win; they should not be allowed to fly their flag, because that entity is no longer in existence.

Angela: I want my history to be respected and my real history to be in the museums and in books. African Americans are a nation of people with a rich heritage; that's the narrative of us hidden in the landscape, a place-specific time and place. Everyone doesn't have the same memory. Education is so important.

How many different formats of writing have been essential for your success?

Angela: I would say the first format that was most essential was poetry. With poetry, I wrote myself out of all kinds of anguish.

My grandmother's narratives have been amazing for me. And, the academic writing to win my scholarship to study abroad; where I lived amongst the ruins and relics and experienced a totally different culture, and was able to take part in the restoration of an icon from the 15th century at The National Center for Research and Cultural Studies an NGO in Old Town Nicosia, Cyprus. This opportunity would never be afforded to someone from my neighborhood who didn't have a Ph D. or was not working at the Smithsonian in the city where I live. Writing got me there as an undergraduate studying for a bachelor's degree!

Judine: You helped to write someone else's history in another country, and now you're helping to write the history where you live.

Angela: Absolutely.

*Never let a problem
to be solved
become more important
than a person to be loved.*

— Barbara Johnson

Allison G. Daniels

Tell us about yourself.

Allison: I'm very energetic and transparent. I am a two-time bestselling author and have published over 31 books. I am also the co-author of over eight books. I wear many hats. I'm a minister, a life coach, a mother of two beautiful queens, and I've been married now for over 17 years. As you can see, I wear many hats. I received the 2016 Bestselling Award from Purposely Created Publishing Company, which published my book titled *Walk in Your Authority, Unleash the Divine Power from Within.*

When did you start writing?

Allison: I started writing around the age of 10 or 11 years old, just writing in my journal, jotting down a lot of things about everyday life. In 1996, my first book came out, a collection of poetry, which is titled *Jesus, A Joy to Call My Own.* I self-published that book, which became the beginning of my publishing journey.

What are your jobs outside of being an author?

Allison: For the past 34 years in Federal government, I have worked as a Lead Paralegal Specialist, Paralegal Specialist, Lead Secretary and more. As an entrepreneur, I am a life coach, helping to bring clarity to the things that people are trying to accomplish, where they may feel stuck. I also help authors get their books professionally printed and published. I help move manuscripts from paper to print. To date, I have coached four authors under my company which is awesome. I plan to launch my publishing company in 2019.

Where can we find your books?

Allison: My books are on my website: AllisonGDaniels.com, Amazon.com, BarnesandNoble.com and BooksAMillion.com.

How many hours a day do you write?

Allison: Normally, I write anywhere between two to three hours a day, in the evenings after work. Once my family is asleep and I've spent the time needed as a mom, as a wife, and as a caregiver, then I set aside some time to write in my office. I have paper and pens set out specifically for that time, and I always begin with an outline.

What family adjustments have you had to make with your writing?

Allison: One family adjustment I have had to make with is learning how to balance things out. My husband and I work well together; we make sure, no matter what is happening, our children's lives are balanced and I'm not all over the place. Let's say on Monday baby girl has something to do or my husband has something to do. I would take care of what I need to do on Tuesday, for us to be on one accord. I know every time I run into someone, somewhere, they mention I'm always busy. But I am also a caregiver for my mom and dad who both live with us. I have another world outside of speaking, which is a blessing, but we've all learned how to try to balance and adjust. And then I take time away for myself. Every January, I go away for a weekend by myself into a hotel to relax and get ready for what the new year will bring.

We all have to pitch in, to make sure everyone has their own time. My husband makes airplanes as a hobby; he enjoys doing that. Outside of helping me and driving me everywhere, he has his own time. I'm a scheduled person; everything has a place, and everything has a time. And if anyone knows me, they know I don't like to be late. I'm always 30 to 40 minutes ahead of time, making sure everything is organized with a checklist. I have signs put up in my home to let everyone know about my upcoming speaking engagements.

What have you found to be the best way to market your books?

Allison: Definitely social media. I'm talking about Facebook, Instagram, and YouTube. I also recommend book signings, conferences, retreats and Anchor for podcasting. I'll record a podcast at nine o'clock at night and then upload it the same day. I do a lot of radio interviews, television interviews, and magazine interviews. I try to stay active and current. I've continued to market myself, because I believe that after you do all of your writing, the next part is marketing yourself, branding yourself, and making sure that your book speaks for who you are. If I haven't conducted myself the right way or if I haven't presented myself the right way, it shows. I always try to be very presentable. I critique myself a lot. But I have to consult God because I can get busy and become out of balance. And if that's not what God told me to do, then I'm not going to do it.

I know specifically that God told me about Facebook live at 5am; I received clarity. I do that every Monday morning. You have to be consistent, then modify it to work for you once you decide that's what you want to do. I try to put up a YouTube video once a week, or at least every month.

Do you prepare the night before for your Monday morning Facebook at 5am?

Allison: I'm glad you asked. I prepare a week or two ahead. I know what I'm going to say, or at least I have the gist of what I'm going to say on Monday. Once I finish one Facebook live at five, I'm preparing for next Monday.

Can anybody follow you on Facebook?

Allison: Yes, on Facebook: allison.g.daniels and YouTube: AGDaniels29.

Did you have to step out on faith with your books?

Allison: I really did. I say that because I had many challenges behind me or against me. Number one was not initially knowing anything about writing or about publishing and how to get started. I had to step out on faith, and I had to trust other people with my writing, which is the hardest thing to do because once you write it, it's your baby. But to release it to someone, you don't know whether or not they're going to have that same care. There were challenges I went through. In 1997, I released one of my book's titled *Black Man, I Love You.* I went back and forth with the printer, because he wouldn't return my books after I made the final payment. I had to kind of fight back and forth with the printer to get my book out of his hands.

I had to eventually get the law involved which was scary for me because I never had to do this before. My contract was signed, products were paid in full and in cash. But what I didn't realize was the printer, or the company, was releasing their book the same month. They didn't want my book to be released at the same time. That was a challenge.

From that experience, I never wanted to trust anyone else with my book. But I thank God that I just never stopped writing, even though that was one of those times where you don't sleep, you're trying to figure out what's the next level and where do I go from here. It still worked out. The book was still released; that was a blessing.

Are you using the same printer for your other books?

Allison: No, I've used several printers and a few publishers down through the years. I've used iUniverse for one book, then I went with Purposely Created Publishing Group for my 31st book. I am very pleased with the owner, Tieshena Davis, and her awesome staff. From the time my book was placed in their hands until the time it was finished, everything just went very smoothly, and I always try to recommend this as a good publishing company.

What was the best money you ever spent as a writer?

Allison: I do a lot of investing in stocks. A friend taught me how to read the *Wall Street Journal* and how to invest in the stock market. Then I started doing it from home. I'm always up between 3:00 am or 3:30 am in the morning, because I'm watching my money and I'm moving things around. I love new shoes and new clothes; I also love to make sure that my money works for me while I'm sleeping.

Does writing energize or exhaust you?

Allison: Writing definitely energizes me. Even when I feel a little exhausted, I just step away from it, but I have to come back because it's my passion. It's my gift and I always tell people that it's my purpose. I've been doing it for so long, I've been walking in it for so long; I know writing is what I'm called to do. I don't let it get so far out of my focus where I don't want to do it anymore, because I know that that is my passion.

Do you ever feel like the words are not flowing?

Allison: Yes, I do have those moments, you know where I'm stuck; you might call it writer's block. But, when I have those days, I pick up another book and just start reading or I play some soft, soothing music. I normally find other things to do until that writing moment resurfaces. I really don't get frustrated with writer's block. I try to look at writer's block as a way of telling me that I just need to settle myself down because I may be doing too much and then my words start flowing all over again.

What lessons have you learned as a writer?

Allison: I've learned many lessons: make sure that you are disciplined; make sure that you stay focused; be aware of the distractions that will come into your life. Even though the distractions come, you have to be able to not overlook them, but go back to the first thing that you started doing, which was writing.

I keep an outline, because when I'm caught off guard with a distraction, I can go right back to the outline and say this is where I stopped, which brings me back to my focus. I've learned to not get discouraged when I can't find the right words. I've learned to not be moved easily. And even though things may come my way, I still try to make sure that I'm not so far off that I can't get back to what I have on my paper.

Distractions are in everyday life. In 2014, my mom was very ill. I don't want to say that was a distraction, that might sound harsh, but that was a point in my life where I could have stopped writing. I could've just pushed everything to the side and given up. But I stayed focused and still maintained my peace in helping her. I knew that may have just been a distraction to stop me from publishing my book, *Walk in your Authority: Unleashing the Divine Power from Within*, which became my first bestselling book out of the 31 books that I have written. Now the storm is over, my mom is healthy, and I thank God that I didn't give up and still released my book in the midst of it all. Maybe it would have been a distraction to the world, but it was a blessing to me and my family.

We may have to shuffle things around, or do things a little differently, but don't let the distractions stop you from pursuing your purpose. You may have to stop what you are doing for a minute; don't give it up. It was an adjustment and a change.

I didn't allow any of that to distract me. You can be overwhelmed at work and have a heavy workload and when you get home, you don't feel like doing anything else. I made it my business that when I arrive at home after a stressful day to not immediately walk into my house. Instead, I sit in my car in the garage for about five or ten minutes and give myself a pep talk to leave whatever happened at work, at work. I don't just jump out of my car and walk in with the work baggage, because then that throws off the whole family foundation. They don't know what I just went through at work and they don't need my negative responses.

When people see me, they think that everything is together; I get that all the time. I try to tell people that I go through the same things that they go through. I go through the same hurt, the same loss, the same disappointments, the same rejections, just in other ways. I handle it differently. I see it differently. I keep moving, you know. I'm glad that my book came out, *Walk in Your Authority: Unleashing the Divine Power from Within* because that's what I had to do in order to move to my next level. It's my testimony. I have a chapter in the book that my mom had to okay to put in there, which is called "Standing in the Midst of the Storm." I was called to be a minister before my mom took sick in July 2014. I was going to be licensed in October 2014. I told God, "Listen, if you make my mom well, I will not answer the call." Then, I went to church and my pastor preached, "Don't attach what's going on in someone else's life to what I have called you to do."

I understood, because I am not responsible for my mother's walk; she's been walking with God all her life.

Knowing this freed me, because I kept asking God, "What did I do wrong?" I thought that it was something that I did or didn't do. I think sometimes when our parents get sick, or even our children, we try to throw it all on us and that's just not what God wants us to do. You're partially connected, but it's their walk.

Do you view writing as a kind of spiritual practice?

Allison: Writing is spiritual and therapeutic for me, because it takes me into another world. When I'm writing, I'm away from everything that's going on around me, and sometimes I'm writing outside of the box. What I may put in my books may be a little bit different than my life, because I'm trying to create another world for myself.

Judine: I just recently read a book titled *One Crazy Summer*, by Rita Williams-Garcia. It's for children aged 9–12 years old, based on one summer vacation. The whole book was the children's adventure. The dad lived on the east coast and sent the three sisters to be with their mom, who lived on the west coast. As I was reading the book, I realized Ms. Williams-Garcia wrote this book with a time span of 30 days. I mention this because a lot of times people might say, "Well I don't have anything to write about. What can I write about?" But you have 365 days of the year, and your life is a continuous stream of activity.

Did you have to substitute events or names in your books?

Allison: I actually did that, because first of all, I just didn't want to mention the name, and I don't believe that I would have received permission, but I wanted to move forward. It was one of those books that I needed to get out, because I knew someone was going through something and they needed to know that no matter what you're going through, you can still face tomorrow, you can still face another day. I wanted them to know the challenges I was facing. I made it through; I made it and I write about it in my book *Facing Tomorrow*.

What are the common traps for aspiring writers?

Allison: The first common trap would be publishing your book before it's edited. An editor can act as a critical reader and help refine the meaning of words. When we are rushing to get our book out, not getting an editor can be a trap, even though it's a good book.

Secondly, we may believe that we all have our own voice and we're the only ones that can tell our own story. But I believe that when we tell our story, let's make sure that it's grammatically correct. Let's make sure that it's error free. Some things you may not be able to catch, maybe a period or something like that. You want to make sure that you have people that are in place, that can speak to you and tell you, "Listen, you know, you're going in this direction, but the book should be going in another direction." We get trapped in our plots. Third, I've seen title that are too long. You want to try and get to the point with your titles.

If you didn't write, what would you do?

Allison: You know, I really don't know. I would love to sing, but I can't sing. But I could learn. I would love to start a teen's empowerment summit. It would be a youth club for young girls to teach them about etiquette, self-esteem, and definitely about writing. I have been focusing on this project called "Diamonds and Leadership." What better place to start than with my own two daughters and then to venture out to help other young ladies.

I have found is that the ideas are constantly flowing. The more that I write, the more that I put out, God fills me up all over again. My vessel is constantly being filled day by day.

How can we learn more about your books and your life coaching?

Allison: I have everything on my website at allisongdaniels.com. I have different packages, because you may need coaching in different areas. You may just need help with getting your book out. Some people need coaching for taking their book to the next level. Some need coaching because they are at a point in life where they want to transition from working a nine-to-five job to be an entrepreneur. Some want to transition from one job to the next job. Some are now experiencing the empty nest syndrome, with the children gone, and need someone to speak with to help with accountability in reaching their next level.

What are the different formats of writing that have been essential for your success?

Allison: I have used free writing to shorthand. I might write poetry, or life stories. I'll write to see what fits for whatever title I'm working on. I always start with a title and I always start with outlines.

Once I have the title and outline, everything starts flowing. Even though I have 31 books published, I'll slow down for a minute. In my file cabinet, I have manuscripts to publish books for the next few years to take me through 2030.

Don't close the book when bad things happen in your life; just turn the page and begin a new chapter.

— LaToya Jackson

Fiction Writer

Cynthia Freeman Gibbs

Tell us about yourself.

Cynthia: I am a native of Lansing, Michigan. I left Lansing to go to college at Florida A&M University in Tallahassee. I completed five internships, two were with a Fortune 500 pharmaceutical company. The company hired me after my graduation, and I began my career. I moved to Des Moines, Iowa and moved up the corporate ladder from being a pharmaceutical representative to a professional development trainer, business manager, and then an account executive. I followed my career to Texas and ended up in San Antonio in 2002.

Now, here I am. I wasn't planning to write a book, but the company had layoffs in 2015. I had a year to basically be a lady of leisure and volunteer throughout the community and in my church. Then in 2016, I went to the library to get a book to read but instead, when I returned to my home, I opened up my laptop and started typing. I actually typed four chapters in three hours, sent it to my family and they told me to keep going because it was good. In four months, I completed the book. And now I am a new author.

What's the title of your book?

Cynthia: It's called *Reasonable Insanity: A Doctor Olivia C. Maxwell Novel.* She is a Clinical Psychologist and readers follow the journey of her life in this book. It can be found in paperback and digital form on Amazon, also in digital format on Barnes and Noble, iBook, and Kobo. Hopefully, it will soon be available in brick and mortar bookstores.

What is your job outside of being an author?

Cynthia: I am 100% author and volunteer. I choose to not go back into the corporate world. Once I began writing, I realized this was a passion. I dabbled with writing years ago but never had the time to really invest in it. It wasn't something where I was just gung-ho to be a writer. Now that I am, I believe this is where I'm supposed to be. I don't see myself doing anything else other than writing and the things involved around writing, such as speaking engagements and workshops.

Where did you get your idea for your book?

Cynthia: I was inspired, unfortunately, through a tragic situation with one of my friends. It made me look at the fact so many women have on a mask and their life looks perfect from the outside. You see educated women working in professional careers. They have a great husband, perfect children, and maybe live a high-society type of lifestyle. Their home is luxurious, and they drive fancy cars, but on the inside, they're dying slowly. Perhaps, they are living in their own personal nightmares. Once I thought about how many people I knew who are living this kind of life, I realized I'd tapped into something not just isolated to one person. That's how I developed this character.

Do you think you, at one time, were the type of woman who tries to make everything look good on the outside, but you were suffering on the inside?

Cynthia: Fortunately, I can't say that's me. However, I have received messages from young women letting me know I am telling their story. Many African American women are able to connect to some of the issues my character, Olivia, has dealt with around relationships with her mother and sister. Olivia is a dark-skinned woman who was raised by a light-skinned family. They treated her differently from how they treated her sister. She has mental illness in her family and has self-image issues where she was basically made to feel she's not beautiful, although she is.

She also deals with bulimia. This is not something you hear people talk about in the African American community. Olivia's mother and boyfriend both told her she was fat. Although she's 5'10" and weighs 135 pounds, her boyfriend suggested she needed to lose ten to fifteen pounds.

These are, thankfully, not my own issues. However, with some of the things she deals with in relationships, there is a little piece of something I may have once thought of doing, but she actually carries out the deed. My advice to people is, don't do what Olivia does. Please don't follow her actions. Sometimes you can reason with your insanity, which is why the title really fits. When people hurt her, she has a way of justifying her actions. It's similar to an old saying, "hurt people, hurt people."

Judine: It sounds like you touched on a lot of different issues within the black community, especially around our melanin. Even though this is residual from slavery, the issue of color still prevails in the black community. In my opinion, we continue to judge one another if your skin is light, medium brown, paper bag brown or dark-skinned. White people don't really care what hue your melanin is, they just look at you as being a black person. It's good you talk about these issues because hopefully we can unify ourselves.

Cynthia: When we look in our community, we can help each other by accepting the way we look. Are we taking the time to say,

"You're beautiful?" Do we recognize when someone has a mask on, but inside they hate the skin they're in? In one of my book club discussions, someone said, "That's me. I've dealt with that with my mother." Or, "I've dealt with it in my community where I didn't feel beautiful because I'm dark-skinned." Hopefully this book generates the conversation to get people to say, "You know what, let's talk about our skin complexion."

Do you think writing can be a part of the healing process?

Cynthia: I definitely think it can be. It was healing for me in being able to put thoughts down on paper I didn't realize I had in my head. It's also interesting to think I can be creative when it's not something I thought was part of who I am. I've created things, but not to the point where it's something I thought anybody else would be interested in. So, I found times where I was just tapping away on my laptop and all of a sudden, I get caught up in the story. My husband even joked about how, at one point, I had to stop typing and say, "Oh my gosh." He asked me, "Are you crying over your character?"

I get very emotional because I thought about the pain I created for my character. Then I realized this is the pain of so many people to where all you can do is pray and lay out on the floor and try to figure out how you're going to get through what you're going through. It's healing to write, but I think it's also healing to read. When you can release and get into somebody else's story, you might also make some connections with what a person is experiencing, whether it's yourself or someone you know.

If you could tell your younger self anything about writing, what would you say?

Cynthia: Just let yourself flow. Don't hold back on the things which are in your mind. As one of my favorite writers, Victoria Christopher Murray said, "throw up on a page." Get it all out of your head.

Don't worry about how it sounds. Don't try to edit it. Just get it out. I would tell my younger self, don't be afraid to try different things. Explore, you know. Don't feel like you always have to be in a certain kind of environment. Live in different places. I never thought I would live in Des Moines, Iowa, but I did. It was a great experience for me, and I learned a lot.

You can take from those experiences, and I'm now able to put some of those experiences in my writing. Also, network with people. Take the time to get to know people. I'm finding as it relates to writing and marketing, you have to be able to activate your network. Expand your network, talk to everybody. That's what I would tell my younger self to do.

How can we contact you?

Cynthia: You can contact me either through my Facebook page or my email address which is cynthiafreemangibbs@gmail.com. I also have a website at cynthiafreemangibbs.com where you can send me a message through my guest book. I made it easy. I'm also on Twitter, Instagram, and LinkedIn.

How many hours of the day do you write?

Cynthia: I have narrowed it down to where I like to write between 1pm and 5pm, which was when I worked on this book. I've tried writing in the morning, but there are so many distractions when I'm starting my day. At the end of the day, I like to have time to spend with my husband. I found the early afternoon to early evening is the time where I can really be focused and free with my writing.

Now that you are not working the "9 to 5", do you have anyone helping you with your book marketing?

Cynthia: My husband is usually with me at my book events. He has made sacrifices to ensure I'm able to follow my pursuit of passion by traveling with me to events, carrying the boxes of books, and handling the money. This is in addition to still working his full-time job. He doesn't miss a beat. He's my rock. He's holding it down and I just love him for that.

What was most challenging about the writing process?

Cynthia: I've found writing a book was the easiest part of the process. The most challenging part for me was submitting query letters to publishers and agents. First do your research to find out who is looking for your genre. Who is open to unsolicited manuscripts? Also, who is open to submissions, period? I really found I had to tailor the query letter. Some of the publishers responded that I am a strong writer, but they were not interested at this time. That's where it's like, oh my gosh, all this hard work I did, and no one is paying attention to this. Do I need to change my query letter? Do I need to change the beginning of my book? I think this is what makes you a professional. Another author told me that basically the rejections make you dig back into your work. I'm so glad I did receive my initial rejection letters because my book today is nothing like the first book I submitted. I threw out some chapters. I refined some things, and it's a better book as a result.

How did you get your book published?

Cynthia: When I found out Victoria Christopher Murray and ReShonda Tate Billingsley had a company called Brown Girls Book Publishing (BGB), I knew I wanted to submit my manuscript to them. At the time, they were accepting submissions, but they were asking for manuscripts of 70,000 words or more. I had 68,000 words. I thought, "Let me see if I can increase my word count." When I got to 70,000 words, BGB was closed to submissions. Now what do I do? As it turned out, I'm a member of Delta Sigma Theta Sorority (Delta) and in 2017 the Deltas were having an event in San Antonio titled "Delta Authors On Tour." I thought, "If only I could get my query letter together, with three chapters, and into Victoria's hand."

BGB cancelled the 2017 event but came back next year in February 2018. The night before the event, the San Antonio Delta committee had dinner with BGB and I was given the opportunity to put my work in their hands personally.

Judine: You kept pursuing your passion even though BGB was closed for submissions.

Cynthia: Yes. At the dinner in 2018, the table was set for a table of 30 people. I arrived early and sat in the middle of the table to hear conversations at both ends, just in case Victoria and ReShonda were at the other end of the table. When they came in, they ended up sitting right across from me. The conversation allowed me give each of them a marketing folder, and ReShonda read it at the dinner table. She looked up and said, "Do you have your completed work you can send to me?" I replied, "I have 73,434 words which I can email to you tonight." The next day at the book club event they invited me to be the newest author of BGB. My book was published in September 2018.

What lessons have you learned as a writer?

Cynthia: Don't give up: Plan, Pray and Polish.

What advice would you give someone considering writing a book?

Cynthia: Put your butt in a seat and write. That's what I've told people. So many people have told me, "Oh, I want to write a book. I'm thinking about it." Well, just sit down. If you're someone who likes to write on a legal pad, then write on a legal pad. If you like to write in a journal, write in a journal. I like to type; I haven't written anything for my book on paper. It's all been typed. Whatever it is, just do it and find out what works. If it's a certain environment that stimulates your creativity, then go to those type of places.

Do you think there are common traps for aspiring writers?

Cynthia: I think one common trap is thinking you can't be a writer. Also, thinking no one would enjoy what it is you're putting down on paper. Another is the time trap. If you haven't been given the gift like I was with the layoff, it would be really difficult to be able to focus. If you have children and a spouse along with your other responsibilities, that can be a trap. You have to figure out when you can write. Whereas for me, yes, I can write in the middle of the day, but everyone doesn't have that opportunity.

Judine: A lot of people don't think they have time to write, or they don't even think they are a writer. They say, "I do have a book inside of me, but I am not a writer." You don't know until you put pen to paper; that's when you have become a writer.

Cynthia: Yes, and I struggled initially with thinking am I a writer or am I an author? I didn't know which one. Some people even told me, you're not an author until you've had something published. It took another author to tell me you are an author even without a published work. It was just me having a personal struggle trying to figure out whether I am really authentic.

What has been the most rewarding experience from your writing?

Cynthia: Seeing the excitement of people when they hear I've written a book. It makes me remember how excited I get when meeting authors. I'm like, "Oh my gosh, people are excited to see I wrote a book." Now that I have a fan base, the feedback I'm getting is exciting. I've received messages on text, email, Facebook. People are connecting with the main character. One of my church members said, "Oh my gosh, I can't stand Dr. Olivia." I asked her what didn't she like about the character? She says, "She's got issues and why did she do that to Savvy, her best friend?" To hear people talking about my book as if they know the characters has been very rewarding.

I've had very fun discussions with people talking about Olivia as if she's their friend. That's what I wanted to see. Also, a friend of a friend in Oregon said, "I have that book as part of my book collection." I thought, "Oh my gosh, somebody has my book and they don't live near Texas." That's also been very eye-opening and rewarding. My thought was always I can't wait to see my book on a bookshelf and to see people holding it in their hands and showing me where they are reading it. Some readers have been in the airport, the doctor's office, or in the hair shop and took a picture with my book while they were there.

How many different formats of writing have been essential for your success?

Cynthia: Writing novels has been essential for my success. I think that's what I'm going to be more drawn to because I like how I can take real-life experiences with things I make up and turn it into a story which can be told with a different twist. I would say novel writing is probably the format I am drawn towards. Even though now I've started a crime story, I think I'm going to stick with writing fiction.

The writer cannot expect to be excused from the task of re-education and regeneration that must be done. In fact, he should march right in front.

— Chinua Achebe

Joy Jones

Tell us about yourself.

Joy: I'm a native Washingtonian, and I still live in Northeast DC.
I love Washington. I love everything about DC, I'm a DC girl forever.
I also love the written and the spoken word. Whether it's performance,
poetry, novels, giving a lecture to students, teaching, doing a teacher
workshop or whatever it is, if it's involving the word, I'll do it. I love
language.

Tell us about your books.

Joy: I have several books and a new book coming down the pike.
My first book was a book on relationships titled *Between Black Women
Listening With the Third Ear*. I worked for DC public schools for many
years and I still do workshops for students, as often as I can get into the
classroom. My second book, titled *Private Lessons: A Book of Meditations
for Teachers*, is to help teachers get through those difficult days of being
in the classroom. The book that has gotten the most attention is a

book for children titled *Tambourine Moon*; it's a picture book. It grew out of stories my father used to tell me when I was a little girl. Those stories are the nucleus for the book and how it came about. I've also been included in a few anthologies of poetry and essays.

The book I'm excited about right now is called *Fearless Public Speaking*. Because I do like speaking and performing and giving lectures and conducting workshops, I decided to put some of my ideas in a book. I thought young people might be the ideal audience. So often I hear adults say, "Oh, I'm so scared of public speaking. Oh, I can't; I'm too embarrassed to get in front of an audience. Oh, I'm so nervous." Even you, Judine, said it before we got started, and you were a little uneasy for a while before you hit your stride. If we can talk to people when they're younger, then maybe when they become adults, public speaking won't be so scary. This book will be published and available on my website in 2019. I'm excited about that.

What are your jobs outside of being an author?

Joy: My day job currently is within the DC public library system. I'm a library associate, which means I do a lot of the same things the librarian does, but my degree isn't in library science. I'm a journalist by education and training. I do a lot of activities to bring people into the library; you can discover all the wonderful books we have there. A lot of people come to the library to use the computers, but the library is a living resource. There's a lot of things to do, and a lot of things to learn. We want you to move beyond the book and the computer to see what else the library can do for you.

One activity we had in September 2018 was a health and wellness fair. We had blood pressure screenings, because hypertension is an issue within the black community. We had information on how to eat better; all of us are always trying to find a way to lose weight. And if you just wanted to have some fun, we encouraged everyone to visit the Francis Gregory Library, on Alabama Avenue between Branch Avenue and Pennsylvania Avenue in Southeast DC.

The Frances Gregory Library has changed a lot since the '70s. David Adjaye, the lead architect for the National Museum of African American History and Culture, designed Frances Gregory. We get architecture students coming in from time to time as part of their studies to examine what he did. People who have heard about the building from out of town, visit the library just to browse and see how he put it together. We invite everyone to visit and take a look as well.

One of the crazy things about working at the library is for somebody to come in and say, "I'm looking for a book. I can't remember the author's name. I don't know the title, but the cover is blue." What has amazed me is I can find the book! That always amazes me. God is clearly channeling through me. I love God. God loves me. That channel is clear.

Where did you get your ideas for the books that you've written?

Joy: Initially, my mother used to read books to me and then she would tell me, "Go to the library and get your own book and read it." She was very key in developing my taste for reading. My father continued to read me books after my mother stopped. I would want him to read a book the same way every single night. He would try to turn two or three pages ahead and skip to the end. I would say, "Oh no, Daddy, you skipped a part." So, he dispensed with the books altogether and started talking about his life, talking about his childhood, talking about his growing-up days. That way I couldn't tell him, "You told it the wrong way." He was talking about himself, teaching about his history that I didn't know. My father grew up in Selma, Alabama, and his life was very rural compared to life in a big city like Washington, DC, which I found fascinating. His life stories became the seed for *Tambourine Moon*, my children's story.

Where did you get the title?

Joy: Frequently, reporters and authors may not choose the title for their work. The editor usually has the last say. *Tambourine Moon* was the editor's choice title, which in this case, I thought that was pretty good. My upcoming book, *Fearless Public Speaking*, was also the editor's choice title. I'm not excited about that it, but I'll live with it. I had another title in mind and I put a poll on Facebook with several titles. I liked the title "When Stage Fright Is Your Friend and Other Things You Need to Know About Public Speaking." I wanted "stage fright" in the title, because as I mentioned earlier, a lot of people are afraid to address an audience and a lot of people do get stage fright. But that was not my experience growing up. I've always liked public speaking; I liked being in plays. I liked being the kid to raise her hand with an answer for the teacher.

Sometimes when I would do these things, people would say, "Well, aren't you nervous?" I'd think, what is there to be nervous about? No, I'm not nervous. Or they would ask, "Aren't you scared?" I always reply, "No, I'm not scared." It wasn't until I was grown that I really understood the question they were asking. Just before I speak, I do get a funny feeling right around in my chest, and it feels like a big ball of energy turning around very rapidly. But as a child, I didn't consider that butterflies or nervousness or fright for me; that was the energy I needed to get the job done. That was the energy I needed to remember my lines in the play. That was the energy I needed to make a dramatic gesture as I was speaking. That was the energy I needed to get the work done. Stage fright is what I call energy. I once was told fear and excitement are the same thing, just at opposite ends of the continuum.

Can writing be a part of the healing process?

Joy: Absolutely. I keep a journal and being able to write about what's going on in my life, particularly the things that are not going well, saves me from having to curse someone out or having to beat somebody up or commit a crime because writing can ventilate those feelings in a safe way. The page is safe, and that helps me to heal emotional, mental, or even sometimes physical trauma. It helps to have a place where I can talk about the details and won't be judged. I think any art form is therapeutic.

Being able to write in the journal and get those ideas on paper, on the page, then that clears the channels when I do encounter people in my real life. I'm more settled and stable and able to deal with the situation. Sometimes, once the channel is clear, I can hear from the Man upstairs about what to do and what to say and how to be.

Judine: We need to write in our journals now, then when we encounter various situations, we're more at peace. We know this is temporary and can say, "Wait until I go home and write in my journal about you."

Do you view writing as a spiritual practice?

Joy: Yes, it is a part of the spiritual routine for me; I feel more connected to my higher power. It allows me to be a clear channel. Occasionally, when I've been writing in my journal about a problem, an insight will come to me about how to handle it while I'm writing. If you would ask me to pray with you right now, I would say, "This is the day that the Lord has made. Let us rejoice and be glad in it." I would use the appropriate, beautiful, flowing language in person. I can tell God in my journal, "Do you know what she did to me? I can't believe that heffa said blah, blah, blah." I can be honest. God and I can talk in a different kind of way because nobody's going to see it. But when I'm talking with you, I have to be a little bit more circumspect and polite.

If you could tell your younger self anything about writing, what would you say?

Joy: I would tell myself to be a little bit more disciplined, to write a little bit more frequently. It's amazing; as much as I hate housework, when I decide I'm going to write, suddenly, the house gets cleaned. Suddenly, I can think of a thousand tasks to do other than the work at hand. I would tell myself to be a little bit more disciplined.

How many hours of the day do you write?

Joy: I write in snatches of time. I'm a morning person. The best time for me to write is in the morning. But have I ever been late for work if I begin writing in the morning? No, I like money, so I make sure the money is straight. Maybe I'm late for some other kinds of appointments, but not late for work. I keep my journal with me, then if I get an idea during the day, I can write it down at that moment. If I do focus on writing, it's most frequently in the morning, but it's not limited to the morning. It depends on what I'm working on, if I have a deadline, or what else is going on in my life.

Do you choose your topics, or do they choose you?

Joy: Both. I mentioned earlier; I like money. Sometimes if I'm assigned a project with a check attached upon the completion, that's a big motivator. But the projects I like the best are those where my idea marinates, maybe for years, before I start writing on it. With *Tambourine Moon*, I had been thinking about those stories over a period of years before I started to write the book. The midwife for the book happened when my cousin Cynthia used to always say to me, "You should write a book about our family." And I'm thinking…poor folks growing up in rural Alabama? I don't see it." But she used to say it all the time. At her urging, I decided to sit down with my father and just ask him in a more formal way some questions about his upbringing.

Once I did that, I wrote an article that was published in The Washington Post, and this was pre-Internet. Because the Washington Post is available in cities outside of Washington, DC, my relatives in Alabama read the article. They were thrilled. My cousin Cynthia said, "See, I told you to write a book about our family." I'm thinking I've exhausted this topic. Meanwhile, I was working on a different children's story, which I sent to an editor. Along with the story, I sent copies of other things I had published to let her know I had a track record, which included the article about my father. The editor wrote back and said, "I didn't like your story, but this article about your father, that was really interesting. Can you make a story out of that?" Like I said, I'm motivated by money. It's just a New York editor saying she liked my story. I said, "Okay, let me focus my attention on this." And that's how *Tambourine Moon* came into existence.

What do you find the most challenging thing about the writing process?

Joy: It's slow, tedious work. When I speak to students, sometimes they seem surprised you don't write a book in a first draft and "boom" it's completed, polished and perfect. You have to write and rewrite. Just like a teacher marks up your papers, when you turn it into an editor, he or she marks up your manuscript, and says, "Let's do it again." Change it, write it, revise it. Editing and rewriting are integral parts of the process. It can't be avoided. The students are a little surprised to find that it's not just a burst of imagination and then a finished book.

How do you feel when an editor edits your work?

Joy: I like having an editor. I want to be edited. In my mind, I'm brilliant and I'm a genius, but at the same time I know that's not true. I want the finished product to be as brilliant and wonderful as possible. That second pair of eyes is what will help it get there. I don't always enjoy having to throw stuff out and rewrite stuff and change things that I thought were fine just the way they were. I appreciate it because it makes for a better result. I don't have an issue with that.

What advice would you give someone considering writing a book?

Joy: Be disciplined; show up as often as you can. My favorite definition of the word discipline is remembering what you want. If you want to lose weight, then when someone offers you the second helping of ice cream, but you have to remember what you really want is to be able to fit into your outfit. Remembering what I want, I can say no to the ice cream. If I want to write a book, that means I have to put some words on a blank sheet of paper over and over again. When someone says, "Hey girl, you want to go shopping?" Well, maybe not because I need to sit down and face that blank sheet of paper, for a finished book. Showing up; being consistent; doing the work; knowing that it's slow and tedious. Sometimes when it has to be done, there's no other way to get it. Writing is work.

What is your writing process like?

Joy: For me silence is important. I need a lot of quiet time. One of my friends, who was a prolific writer, told me she did not own a television, and I have to say the TV has been a big time-stealer for me. In today's day and age, being willing to go on an electronic fast, no television, no Facebook, no internet, or having them in very limited doses, opens my imagination and allows me to hear myself more clearly. Most people shudder at the thought of putting down their telephone, but it yields a lot of benefits if you can do it. When I was teaching, in one class the kids had to write a play, which is a fairly big project. Early on some kids would say, "I can't think of anything to write. I don't know what to say. I don't have any ideas." And I would say turn off the television; get off the computer.

Eventually I made turning off the television a regular requirement of the class, having them commit to four days in a row without any electronic entertainment, and their parents had to sign it. I also gave them a list of things to do other than play on the computer and look at TV to occupy their time. Then they had to not only write the play, but also had to write their experience about what it felt like to go without the electronics. Here's the most interesting outcome: there was a parent who used to tell me she liked to write, and she wanted to write a book. When I gave this assignment, she says "Oh, do you have to make it like that? Because you're punishing the whole family."

When we have to monitor him to not watch TV, that means we can't watch TV." And I said, "I'm sorry. It's just four days in a row-no TV or computers." Then one day the same parent accosted me in the parking lot as I was leaving school. She says, "Guess what? I started an article." It was the result of her having to go without the electronics in order for her son to go without and complete the assignment. Being without electronics can be hard. It can drive you up a wall at first, but it's worthwhile if you can pull it off.

What are the common traps for aspiring writers?

Joy: Not showing up for the work. Having delusions of grandeur. Thinking they're going to make a zillion dollars as a bestselling author. Do it because you like writing, because you have something to say. Don't write because you think you're going to get rich. Maybe you will, but in case you don't, do it because it is satisfying.

What is the best way to market your books?

Joy: I'm still trying to answer that question. Not being afraid to kick-start the audience, talking to people. Writing about something other people are interested in, besides yourself. Some writing is just for you, some writing is for the public; authors need the ability to discern which is which; that goes a long way.

I especially like speaking to groups - leading workshops, giving speeches, book signings. When you write, you're alone with your thoughts. And when a reader picks up a book, that's usually a solitary experience, too. But when the reader and writer are in the room together, that's a dynamic exchange.

When marketing, I think it's important not just to think about making a sale but creating an experience. When the person feels something as a result of their encounter with you or your ideas, he or she will want to take home a souvenir of the experience and then they'll buy the book.

Judine: You are available on a website for anyone to contact.

Joy: Yes, my personal website is JoyJonesOnline.com and my arts organization, The Spoken Word, is at TheSpokenWordOnline.org.

What other activities are you involved in?

Joy: In addition to writing, one of the other things I do for fun is Double Dutch. The group is called DC Retro Jumpers and we jump all over DC. In September 2018, we were invited to do a goodwill tour in Russia for 10 days, traveling to Moscow, Saint Petersburg, and Belgorod. We performed for the American Ambassador in Russia, also in schools, orphanages, and musical festivals. Teaching them to do Double Dutch is not a thing where you just sit and watch, you're going to get in the rope and do it too.

Judine: I've compared the Double Dutch rope to a pen because both are a very simple objects, which give great results.

Joy: Robin Epps, who is the lead instructor, has a process where she instructs people to bunny hop, while she positions them. She'll have marks on the ground where you should be, and you see the shock on the kid's face that suddenly, they're there in the rope. I love it the most when adults jump. Women will stand on the side and see us turning, and I can see the look on their face like they want to try jumping. They want to say, "Oh I'm too old." But they look at us and they can't use that excuse.

Eventually, a woman will edge a little closer and we'll ask, "Did you want to jump?" And eventually she'll say yes. It might be a woman who jumped as a kid and it hasn't done it in 10, 20, or 30 years. It might be someone who has never jumped Double Dutch, but always wanted to learn. It doesn't make a difference. We teach her how to bunny hop. Then she's in the rope, and the wig is falling off; she has thrown off her heels. She doesn't care, because she's going forward. I enjoy watching that transformation and the joy infuse her whole body and those endorphins start kicking on the inside, which are the natural feel good chemicals that your body produces, similar to getting high. It's just wonderful to watch that change.

How can we find out more about your books?

Joy: I have a website at JoyJonesOnline.com, where you can learn all about my books. I have a presence on Facebook, under Joy Jones, where I post things that I'm doing. Right now, Instagram is my most interesting outlet for reaching people. It's a challenge to constantly find a picture to tell the story. Let me know how well I'm doing; I'm at #joyjones1433.

What is your most rewarding experience in writing?

Joy: I don't know if I have one that stands out; there have been a number of experiences. Writing *Tambourine Moon*, which was a way of sort of saying thank you to my father for giving me a love of stories. Writing *Private Lessons: A Book of Meditations for Teachers* was also a rewarding experience. My mother and my grandmother were teachers. Writing has been a way of saying thank you to them for teaching me how to read.

How many different formats of writing have been essential to your success?

Joy: All of them. All of them. All of them. Poetry, prose, fiction, nonfiction, theater. And cookbooks; I can't cook, but I read those too. The format doesn't make a difference. I love language.

*Reading is like breathing in;
writing is like breathing out.*

— Pam Allyn

Christian Writer

Kevin Wayne Johnson

Tell us about yourself.

Kevin: My life ministry is developing individual and organizational operating excellence. I coach in order to coax audiences to live out their gifts, and in the words of my national best-selling book series, to then *Give God the Glory!* This book series has earned me, a former radio and television host, 19 literary awards. Gayle King, an editor-at-large for *O, The Oprah Magazine*, has praised my work writing to me, "Your book, Kevin, touched me."

I deliver training on the elements of dynamic relationships, to equip teams with the attitudes and attributes needed to develop individuals into leaders. I do this through motivating workshops, seminars, insightful keynote speeches and compassionate coaching – all to encourage personal and professional growth. As an independent certified coach, teacher and speaker with the nationally recognized John Maxwell Team, I lead learning experiences that are tailored to meet the specific needs of the audience, to help maximize efficiency, growth, awareness and effectiveness. I invite those in the audience to "Put Your Dream to the Test" and provide them with a step-by-step action plan for making those dreams come true. This essential exposure to personal development techniques includes guided study and the practical application of John Maxwell's proven leadership methods.

What formats have you found successful with marketing your products?

Kevin: I would say it's a mixture of a lot of different things. It's a combination of in-person appearances, word-of-mouth advertisement, print media, and social media. It's multifaceted. I haven't found one thing that works as a stand-alone marketing tool. I've even tried hiring PR specialists, but it's been hit or miss. I've applied some of what I've learned through my own reading and research, as well. I probably do more in-person appearances than the average author. I am a people person and that really works well for me. That's how I get invited to a lot of different events and that's how I get in front of people and communicate this message. It's a combination of all those good marketing products.

What kind of research did you do before you started writing?

Kevin: Well, as it relates to my writing, I did two quick pieces of research. Number one, I researched my first and last name, Kevin Johnson. It is a common name and I found out about 17 years ago, when I started writing, there was another Kevin Johnson, a children's book author. I didn't want my name to be mistaken for that Kevin Johnson. To avoid any confusion, I include my middle name everywhere – Kevin Wayne Johnson.

Secondly, when the Lord gave me the title for the book, *Give God the Glory!*, I researched the title for any similar, already published titles.

I searched Amazon.com and did not see any other title by that name other than Mahalia Jackson's song; that was it. The *Give God the Glory!* series was birthed after I published the first book. We're up to eight titles in the series, sold in different languages around the world. I had to do that initial research because God knew something before I did. I didn't know one book would be turned into a series. I was just writing one book.

My books are birthed from my ministry. Ministry was a call that started my initial research. God will keep messing with you until you answer the call.

What lessons have you learned from being an author or being in ministry?

Kevin: The biggest lesson for me is understanding people because we all have different backgrounds and different education levels. We think differently. We process information differently. We were raised in different households. We were raised in different regions of the country. People from New York don't have the same mannerisms as people from Louisiana. It's all in the understanding of one another. Understanding people has been the biggest growth area for me, both in the workplace as a mid-level and senior-level leader, in the ministry and then as an author, because ultimately people are our customers and we have to understand them.

I gave an example one morning in church, to explain how we live in a society, a country, a nation, where there's a lot of animosity in the atmosphere and people are really, really bent out of shape.

This particular day, the right lane of traffic was closed because of construction and the drivers in that lane had to merge to the left lane. The driver nearest me in the left lane did not want me to merge in front of him. When I did, he told me about myself. Now my windows were up, and I didn't hear what he said, nor did I engage in the rhetoric.

However, I wondered what was going on in that driver's mind that would make him so upset. As soon as we got past the construction, I merged back over in the right lane. He continued in the far-right lane to make a turn at the light. Before turning, he stopped, rolled his window down and told me a few words. Oh, I didn't hear what he said; I didn't engage him. But I wonder why people do that.

Judine: Thank you for sharing your example with the driver. It sounds like you were sending love as a healing to that other driver. Even though the driver might not realize it, there's a healing you were sending. That's healing to him through your love, by not reacting.

Kevin: I'll tell you what was on my mind when that was happening. I was reminded of was the incident in Texas where a father and son had an altercation with their neighbor because neither could agree on how to dispose of a mattress. The father and son wanted the neighbor to put the mattress in the alley, but the neighbor put the mattress in a dumpster. Both sides continued to argue and finally the father shot and killed the neighbor.

Judine: Your example reminded me of the Florida fatal shooting because of a parking spot. The first man entered a convenience store, while his family waited in a handicapped parking spot. A second man pulled into the parking lot, and started yelling at the family man's significant other, because of where the car was parked. The first man exited the convenience store and pushed the second man, who then fell to the ground. The second man pulled out his gun and shot and killed the family man. The law is called "stand your ground." But I did hear that the second man had charges against him for manslaughter. That could have been resolved without a fatal reaction. Just sending love to the person can help, because hurt people, hurt people. When somebody does hurt you, you must realize they're coming from a hurt place.

Would you say writing is essential for success?

Kevin: Writing is one of many successful venues to deliver a positive message and to make the world a better place. I think it's through our writing that other doors open and we can selectively walk through because every hour is not promised to us. At the end of the day, it's all about helping this world. Yes, the world would be a better place if we used our gift of writing. As we improve our craft, other doors will open, as it has for me, in ministry, the workplace, and other avenues.

I look at you, Judine, and what you're doing with your radio program and the number of people that you're reaching with a very positive message. Your countenance has been one of love. My blessings have also come from the number of brothers and sisters I have reached across the globe because I said yes to the assignment to tell people that God is good. I have brothers and sisters in different countries all around the world, as a result of just writing one book 17 years ago. Our accomplishments help touch people in ways we will never know.

How long did you work for someone else before you became a business owner?

Kevin: I started my government career as a young man, barely making enough to survive. After 15 years into my career, I was on a dual path. I wanted to be a senior executive. But right around that time when I came to the fork in the road, God called me. Quite frankly, to me the decision was very easy, to become a senior executive, and begin my ministry as God called me to do. I took the dual path, instead of choosing one occupation over the other. I became bi-vocational when I started my ministry work. God started my ministry training and development. Within two years, the first book was published in the *Give God the Glory!* series. It all came together. I chose to remain employed with the Federal government, because I knew I could keep my secular career by taking advantage of all the leadership training.

I attended frontline leadership, mid-level leadership, and senior executive training. This training transitioned over into ministry because church members also need leadership training.

When I was a young man, just beginning my government career, all of my sons were babies. By my 25th and 30th year mark, I had been pouring back into the next generation in the Federal government, which also spilled over into my ministry. God gave me the wisdom to remain gainfully employed for 34 years of government service. It's 2018, and my sons are 20, 21, and 22 years old. The years flew by with learning how to balance family, work and the ministry. The dual track was challenging for many years; however, I was able to make it work because of the work-life balance.

What advice would you give to the person that has a 9 to 5 job and wants to write a book? Some people say, "I'm going to wait until I retire to start writing." That's not bad because, it's their journey.

Kevin: There's not necessarily a best time of day or a certain time in your life to begin writing. Depending on how bad you want to write, you learn to say no to some activities that you're engaged in, then you can have the time to write. If I can do it, then anyone and everyone can do it. It can be done, but you just have to stop some things to make the time to start your writing. It's time management.

Who are your favorite authors and how did they influence your success?

Kevin: Doctor Myles Munroe, founder of the Bahamas Faith Ministry International. I read one of his books in 1993, *Understanding Your Potential: Discovering the Hidden You*, right around the time that I entered into ministry. It's a nonfiction book, which resonates with me. It dives into who you are and helps you pull out the potential that's in you; you can live out your dreams and aspirations and goals. Although Dr. Munroe is no longer living, his legacy lives on through his books. There's something about his writing that touched me, helped to change me, and developed me into who I am today.

Judine: I always knew I would write a book, but before I started on that journey, I read all of Og Mandino's books; they are very inspirational. He's an unsung hero, he really is.

Does a big ego help or hurt?

Kevin: It depends. Some people just have that type of personality that kind of keeps them going. Some people have to be careful, because that ego can turn into pride and pride is one of our downfalls. We have to be very humble because James 5:10 (NIV) states, "Humble yourselves before the Lord, and he will lift you up." It's a very delicate walk. Now having competence and boldness is good, but you have to keep that ego in check. Sometimes it's easy to think you're a little bit better than you are and the fall would be quite hard.

What advice would you give to aspiring writers?

Kevin: What works well, and the advice that I give to people, is to network, network, network. Get to know people and have them to get to know you for the right reasons. When you meet people and you share your vision and something clicks, they can help you to get to where you're trying to go. I like the quote by John Heywood, "Many hands make light work." You can cast the vision, but you may not be able to make it come to fruition by yourself. When you surround yourself with likeminded people, they can definitely help you to get wherever you are headed. I love being an entrepreneur because I get to attend different events and meet people and exchange information. With the person who follows up with me, things begin to happen for the both of us.

With the people who don't follow up with you, you can follow up with them a little bit later. There might be a reason why they didn't call you. I've learned from a number of my mentors to network, network,

network; it pays dividends. A lot of times when you're networking, that person might not even know that in their conversation with you, they are helping you with something else that you might have had in the back of your mind. That's the benefit of talking to many different people. You have your own culture, but you can incorporate the culture from other people in order to help you to be more relatable on a broader scale.

How many different formats of writing have been essential for your success?

Kevin: One book, the print version of my first book, has been essential to my success. Here's the story: In 2000, I published *Give God the Glory! Know God & Do the Will of God Concerning Your Life*. About 10 years later, we added additional content, changed the cover, and made it available in different formats, such as an ebook on Amazon Kindle. It continues to be our best-seller. From this one book, I expanded the content to five different areas for five new titles. Many people ask, "Can you come speak about your book?" Writing speeches has provided another successful format.

In summary, one book generated seven additional titles or additional streams of income. Having multiple streams of income has always been a dream, an aspiration, and a goal. We're not going to reach everybody, but the audience that God does give us to make a positive influence into their lives, makes this world a much better place. When you encourage your readers to go out and make a positive influence on other, then before you know it, you have reached thousands, perhaps millions of people, because they have influenced many more people. This is true networking.

When I attend conferences, people come up to me and they've said, "Do you remember me?" I've replied, "Well, I'll be very honest. I do not." The person usually doesn't get offended, but continues to say,

"You taught me such and such at a previous conference." Again, I put my ego to the side and feel good that I responded to the assignment of sharing God's message.

Judine: I'm going to end with Proverbs 27:17 (NIV) "As iron sharpens iron, so one person sharpens another." We sharpen others with our networking and sharing our tests and testimonies.

Kevin: Amen to that!

*Write it down on real paper
with a real pencil,
and watch shit get real.*

— Erykah Badu

Janice Boss

Tell us about yourself.

Janice: I am thankful to God and I am honored to be interviewed. I am the third child born to Richard and Doris Chatman, and I graduated from West High School in Denmark, Tennessee. I continued my higher education with a bachelor's degree from Lane College in Jackson, Tennessee, and a master's degree in Business and Public Administration from Southeastern University in Washington, DC. I retired from the Federal government after 37 years with my final years working at the U.S. Department of Education.

I've volunteered at the White House under President Obama's administration, coordinated Black History Month programs at the U.S. Department of Education, and hosted the Tuskegee Airmen as participants during the Blacks in Government programs.

As the President of Blacks in Government, Greater Memphis chapter, I have spearheaded annual youth oratorical competitions, and various outreach activities for the youth in the community. Finally, I am a proud member of the Delta Sigma Theta Sorority, Beta Chi Chapter.

Can an author survive on book writing alone?

Janice: I would say some probably can maintain their standard of living from book writing alone. I thought before I became an author that a person could have writing as their main job for income. However, after doing my research, I have discovered, and learned as being an author, that writing is just a by-product on your journey in life. Even Hemmingway had a job and almost all popular authors have another source of income. Furthermore, even some of the authors on the New York's best sellers' list do not hit the million-dollar mark. Only one percent of all authors make enough money to live on without another source of income.

Judine: J.K. Rowling is a good example because even though she is making money from the Harry Potter books, there's residual money from the movies, as well. Yes, she probably could survive on those book sales alone; however, she continues to put her published works for sale in different formats.

Where did you get the ideas for your book?

Janice: I have always been a people's person. I love people and being a part of organizations. When thinking about writing a book, God began to speak to me and he said, "You love relationships and you're always talking about relationship building." No matter where I am, even in a church, I think that it is important for leaders to always encourage and help build good relationships. I am relationship builder, even in my family, that's why I was inspired to write my first book *Code to Human Life: Building Good Relationships*. I would also like to thank Jesse Sharpe, my publisher, for actually committing to our schedule for publishing the book on time.

Do you have any other jobs?

Janice: I'm a business entrepreneur, and a business health and wellness consultant, and that's what I love doing. I'm all about health, and of course I live by the Le'Vive juice. I am 67 years old taking no prescription drugs. I just love to talk about health and wellness, and I have a passion for it, as well. That's the business that I continue to do. I keep myself healthy, as I write.

How can writing be a part of the healing process?

Janice: I feel God gives us the vision to write. Sometimes we are procrastinators and we might put it off and continuously put it off. I know that for me, when I published the book after three years of writing, I was at peace with myself. As I was writing the book *Code to Human Life: Building Good Relationships*, I only told one brother who motivated me to finally publish the book. I feel God has really done a work in my life after completing this book.

If you could tell your younger self anything about writing, what would you tell her?

Janice: I would say, "Stop procrastinating. Stop making up excuses. Stop saying, 'I'm going to take some training courses before I begin to write my book.'" You have to get started and sometimes it's very difficult to get started in the writing process. However, it's a must that you say to yourself I will just pray over it, and then say, "I'm going to do this."

What do you think causes the procrastination?

Janice: I think writer's block can cause procrastination. We all can write, but it takes time to write books. It's not something that you can just do overnight; it takes a lot of concentration. We all have different processes as authors. In order to complete my book, I literally had to say to myself, "I'm going to work at least three hours a day;" and I did that every single day, for a couple of months. After three years, mind you, the book was completed.

Judine: For that person who doesn't like to write, writing is like a necessary chore. For example, the trash needs to be taken out and you must do it. You have to start with taking out that first bag of trash, and then it becomes a habit.

Janice: God and the Holy Spirit lead me every single day and coach me in what to do and how to do it. I have been a writer in my career all my life, but I never even thought about becoming an author. After God prompted me to begin writing the book, I really wanted to help other people to self-publish their own books and to become authors. I started out going around with my publisher to help other people. God wants us to help other people walk in their purpose. This is actually how I started to really think about writing a book, becoming an author, by thinking how I can help others with their life experiences.

Judine: I like the fact that you know you have always been a writer. A writer is not really a job title; it's something that everyone has to do. But then you transitioned and said, "I want to become an author." Now that's your title, being an author. Thank you for making that distinction.

What do you find the most challenging about the writing process?

Janice: I find having the time to write and actually writing are two different things. I learned years and years ago, that brainstorming is the first source of God speaking to you. I believe that's the reason why it took me a while deciding to be an author. I was still brainstorming and thinking things over in my life. After I felt in my spirit that God was really telling me to become an author, then I began to put the ink to the paper, and I knew God was speaking to me. Writing a book is a by-product of your writing.

What lessons have you learned as an author?

Janice: I have learned a lot about how God speaks to me. We all have a destination, and we all have a purpose; eventually we will walk in that purpose. I feel God was guiding me to walk in my purpose as an author, since I was already writing. However, there were some things that I probably should have spent more time on while writing my book, one of which was getting editors up front. I thank God for my editors; they were very helpful. I find lots of people who are wanting to become authors, who will say, "No, I can edit my book myself." It's almost impossible to edit your own writing. I know for my next book I will spend more time on editing my work. It takes research to find the right editor. This is one lesson that I learned, ensuring that I enlist the right editors first, before going to the printer.

I've also learned marketing is a very important part of the publishing process. Before I even wrote my book, I thought about marketing, because I helped a young man who had published close to 20 books. I began to tell him, "We need to market these books." I helped him distribute the autographed books as Christmas presents to leaders in his community. Before we knew it, other people had purchased the book. That's when I learned when you give your autographed book to a leader, it really takes on a new marketing position.

Judine: I've used the saying writing is 1% of the time, publishing is 10% of the time, and marketing is 89% of the time that you have to spend on your book. It is very important to market your book before you publish to get a following. People will know that you're entering the book industry, that your book is about to be published, and they can be prepared to buy it. The initial marketing window is about six months after publication and to maximize that six months, you need to start marketing before you have published your book.

How did publishing your first book change your writing process?

Janice: There are a lot of things that I would change in hindsight, for example, we just mentioned talking about the marketing process ahead of time. When I was doing my writing, I didn't really want anybody to know about my book, because what if I don't finish the book? I thought of people in my life who have started projects years ago, and they were really on top of becoming an author, but they never completed the project. I think I had some fear about not finishing. Getting credible sources to write reviews of my next book, and even marketing by writing reviews for other books, these are activities I'm going to do for my next book.

Judine: After I published my book, I wrote four book reviews per month for one year, and the Midwest Book Review published them. Goodreads is another site that accepts book reviews. Writing the book reviews helped to market my name, even though I didn't put the title of my book in the tagline.

What is the best way to market your books?

Janice: You definitely have to market using word of mouth. However, I also have had a lot of good things happening at conferences. I love attending conferences. Once I wanted my book to be published before a specific conference, because I wanted to take 20 books with me for networking. When I got to the conference, all of the books were sold in one day. I thought to myself, "I should've taken 100 books." I just find that if you're a member of various groups, for example AARP (known as the American Association of Retired Persons) or a Greek organization, those are venues to market and sale your books. In addition, going back to your alma mater for homecoming games is another good avenue for marketing.

Judine: I like how you mention it's better to bring more books and take some home, than to bring a smaller amount and have people walking away without your book. There is a chore in carrying your books everywhere you go; however, the benefit is that you have them for sell at any place, and any time. Otherwise, if the reader isn't face to face with you, the likelihood goes down that they will purchase your book.

Janice: I always attend the Congressional Black Caucus Annual Opening every year at the Walter E. Washington Convention Center, in Washington, DC. Once, there was a young man coming down the hallway with his books and he said, "I just finished speaking on my book." I said, "Really, well what is it about?" After hearing that, my former colleague and I bought his book and got his information. I then told him, "I'm an author too." He asked if I had my books with me, and I was able to reach down in my bag and sell my book to him.

What was your most rewarding experience from writing your book?

Janice: One of my most rewarding experiences is being interviewed on the "By Any Ink Necessary Program." Sometimes, as an author, or any profession where we are honored, we can take it lightly, and I don't want this to be my case. At other times, I will see people, and they'll say to me, "Janice, I didn't know you were an author, where are your books?" I remember being at an oratorical competition, and the members heard that I was an author, and they said, "We have to buy your books, just because we know you."

Another example is when I sent a former colleague information about my book by email, and she forwarded the email to people in different offices of the agency where she worked. This type of experience touches my heart when that happens, knowing it's nothing but God that causing this to happen. Soon afterwards, I received an email asking when I could speak at my former colleague's office about the book. Those kinds of experiences, I just know are nothing but God. I thank and give honor to God, and I'm very humbled by these types of occurrences.

How many different formats of writing have been essential for your success?

Janice: After brainstorming and planning, I put my fingers to the keyboard or put ink to the paper.

My aim is that my art will touch peoples' hearts, because if you can touch them, their consciousness, you can shift their behavior into action.

— Liza Jessie Peterson
"The Peculiar Patriot"

Nonfiction & Instructional Writer

Judine Slaughter

(Interviewed by K. Jones)

Tell us about yourself.

Judine: I'm the founder of the United Black Writers Association, Inc. The need for the organization arose because I didn't see many people of color presenting at writer's conferences, sharing their stories and resources. For many years in America, it was illegal for Black people to read or write. Some are suffering the residual pain, thinking they are not worthy to put their words into print. You are worthy; you've always be worthy.

I am a nonfiction and technical writer. *Clear Skinned* is a collection of letters and *Do It Yourself Publishing/Write from the Spirit* is an instructional book on how to use the Internet resources for publishing. It can be done, because I did it.

How did writing a nonfiction book affect your relationship with your mother?

Judine: *Clear Skinned* is a compilation of letters exchanged with my eldest child's father, before my first pregnancy. I don't mention my mother by name or anyone else's name directly. My name and his name are the pet names we had for each other, and my daughter's name is a moniker she gave to herself. In the letters, I struggled with telling my mother about my feelings about my first relationship.

After I published the book, my mother and I continued to have a good relationship. I think maybe both of us had to reevaluate our relationship after reading the letters. She never got mad, or anything of that nature. There's never been time where we stopped talking because of certain events. That's one thing that has been good about our relationship. We have applied the motto of "agree to disagree."Anybody who knows her who read my book, would know exactly who I'm talking about, but she's never voiced her disapproval of the book.

For example, when my son was in seventh grade, he had to write an autobiography. He shared his draft with me and asked for help selecting the pictures. When I read it, I could feel his sadness when he mentioned how his father and I had divorced. Learning of his emotional injuries from the divorce was tough for me to digest. I helped him type it, yet I questioned "Did I do a good job as a mom?" I tried to suggest for him not to mention certain events, but he wanted to keep his words. Knowing the importance for him to tell his truth, I didn't make any edits. He doesn't know I saved his autobiography, because this is his first book. I love him for being brave enough to put his words down in print and being honest in it.

Did you have to step out on faith with your first book?

Judine: Yes, I did step on faith, because my daughter's birth father, Ralph, did not know that I was putting the letters together. But before

I even started collecting the letters, he told me that I would write a book because he had seen me free writing for many years when we worked together at Circuit City. I worked in the movie room and he would write me short messages on the back of the equipment price tags. Or he would put cards around the store, and I had to find them. Then one day he asked, "Are you saving the notes?" I honestly didn't see any need to save them. He then told me one day I would write book. I started saving every scrap of paper with his words, and as God would have it, I saved the drafts of the letters I wrote to him. That's how I could have the exchange of his letters and my letters in the book *Clear Skinned*.

Several months before publishing *Clear Skinned*, I learned Ralph was visiting his mother in Calvert County. I said, "Rebecca, did you want to go on a mission?" She agreed, and we drove down to the grand-mother's house, knocked on the door, and they did not answer. We did see the curtains move and we saw a car in the driveway. She wanted to stay, so she stepped out on faith by staying at the house on the back patio, while I drove back up the road for an appointment. Eventually he opened the door. When I picked her up, he agreed for his letters to be in the book. She stepped out on faith because she stayed outside of the house until he opened the door. This happened during the summertime, while the weather amiable.

What are your jobs outside of being an author?

Judine: Outside of being an author, I work for the Federal Aviation Administration. On Fridays in 2018, I started attending the Dinner and Movie event at the ELife Restaurant in Capitol Heights, MD.

Al-Qamar Malik is the host, and one evening she mentioned ELife was offering studio time for $25 an hour if you purchased 13 shows. Initially, I brushed it off. On the next Friday, Al-Qamar again announced the discounted studio fees. God inspired me to say to myself, "I could be a radio host." The United Blacks Writers Association met monthly for five years at the Karibu bookstore before it closed, and we haven't had face-to-face activities since that time. I accepted the call for this different avenue to interview writers/authors.

It's not difficult to give the interviews. Being extremely introverted, I felt out of my comfort zone by the third show. The 60 minutes can seem like six hours if you are uncomfortable with being in front of the camera. But I had to continue with the show, because I had already lined up a list of writers to interview. After the 13th show, I became more comfortable talking with viewers watching.

How many hours of the day do you write?

Judine: I write whenever I pick up a pen, which is whenever I have time to sit and think. I'm unusual as I can free write about anything on my mind at any time of the day. I can fill up the page with words in a very short span of time. It amazes me how quickly I can dump my thoughts on paper. Whenever I have the urge to write, I'm scrambling around looking for a blank sheet of paper. But if I've got a pen in my hand, I'll will write on a napkin or any scrap of paper.

It's not that I'm writing anything specific, I'm just free writing my thoughts, trying to stay positive. Depending on how much space I have, I'll start with the Lord's Prayer or Psalms 23 as an opening devotion. I like to take different color pens and see the hues blend together like a mosaic. Because I write so much, I constantly need blank paper around me.

What was the best money you've ever spent as a writer?

Judine: The best money that I spent was on PageMaker publishing software, which in 2002 was then $500. I needed PageMaker to format the two books published by my publishing company at that time, RAH Distributors. Because I didn't want those expensive CDs sitting on my front porch, I had them delivered to my job, a government building. The day of delivery was the day of the anthrax scare. Eventually I received the software and formatted the two books for the printer.

Does writing energize or exhaust you?

Judine: Free writing energizes me. I'm allowing God to give me more thoughts, more ideas. But if I need to write a paper for school, that can initially exhaust me. When complete, I'm energized.

What lessons have you learned as a writer?

Judine: As a writer, I've learned the written word has power. You can talk and talk, but those words evaporate. When you put your words down in ink on paper, these words penetrate. I think I learned this very early in life.

When I was in the 12th grade, my mother and I would occasionally watch Robert Schuller's "Hour of Power" on Sunday mornings. For one service he says something along the lines of, "If somebody is bothering you, write me a letter about it." I wrote a letter to Robert Schuller about my mother. I don't remember where I put the letter, but she came to me and she said, "I read your letter." There was nothing I could say. She wasn't mad, but I felt she became friendlier to me. When I put the letters together for *Clear Skinned*, this was a second iteration of her reading something that I had written about her.

Often people disregard my verbal words, I guess because I don't sound forceful. If I'm letting you know how I feel and the receiver doesn't listen, or if I feel as if there's no action, I won't say too much more. I've learned to put my thoughts on paper and people pay more attention.

What are some of the common traps for aspiring writers?

Judine: I think the most common trap for aspiring writers is not writing or not believing they are a writer. Just write it; just write it down. Don't worry about grammatical mistakes, just write it. There are so many opportunities where you can publish your manuscript for just one book. It's really a galley, especially if you don't have a formal cover. Many people are trapped for perfection. And it only takes one book to make you an author. If you pick up a pen and put your words on paper, you are writer.

If you could tell your younger self anything about writing, what would it be?

Judine: I think it's important to write how you feel, because a lot of times we silence ourselves; we don't want to hurt anybody. We don't want our feelings to cause any problems, and we lock up our feelings. It's like we sacrifice ourselves. We lay ourselves on the table and allow ourselves to be the sacrifice for the sake of other people. Stop sacrificing; stop the silence. Tell your truth.

How did publishing your first book change your writing process?

Judine: Publishing my first book changed my writing process by making me more aware of tightening my language and getting someone to edit my work. I've heard and believed to be true, "Every writer needs an editor." Editing only improves your writing. No matter how well you know the content, you should get someone to proofread your words.

What are your other books?

Judine: I would be remiss not to mention being a contributing author in an anthology project titled *Weary and Will*, with Sheryl Kiser Jackson as the main author. This was her baby; she's a high school English teacher, and she did an excellent job in editing my story.

However, you can just now take anything and make one book. For example, I've used a site called Chatbooks.com and published one book of photos from my cellphone. That's pretty cool, especially for anyone who has too many pictures on their phone, and they run out of storage space. You have the option to put the pictures on your laptop, which I have done, but you can also consolidate them into a book. I also have five yearbooks from my Facebook posts. Whenever I am feeling a certain way, I read my Facebook books. This is my narcissism.

Who helped with your success?

Judine: First and foremost, I'm grateful the Creator guides my steps every day. Then my family has helped me with my success, with their positive motivation of my endeavors great and small. Third, I want to thank all the people I have worked with at the Federal Aviation Administration. They have helped me find my inner strength and provided avenues for me to use my creativity. Last but not least, there are the people who have agreed to be interviewed for the "By Any Ink Necessary" show. I've known many of them for years; they have helped me become a better version of myself.

The people we surround ourselves with either raise or lower our standards. They either help us to become the best version of ourselves or encourage us to become a lesser version of ourselves. No man becomes great on his own. No woman becomes great on her own. The people who surround us help determine our fate. We need all types of people in our lives, positive and negative, who raise our standards unknowingly or on purpose, remind us of our essential purpose with their negative words or encouraging words, and in the end challenge us to become the best versions of ourselves.

What is the best way to market your book?

Judine: I have found being a member of writing organizations is the best way to market your book. The United Black Writers Association was birthed from the Black Writers Guild in MD. I initially began attending their workshops in Baltimore to help my daughter market her book. Writing organizations will have conferences or advertise book fairs where you can sell your book. And membership allows you to network with other authors. Often authors-in-training ask, "How can I write a book?" If you are a member of a writer's organization, even when you might not have all the ducks in a row, you can ask the other members for help, because probably they too were once in a position where they need help. After a year in the Black Writers Guild, MD, I asked to initiate a chapter in Prince George's County. I wrote a proposal and they agreed. Three years later, I changed the name to the United Black Writers Association, Inc.

How many different formats of writing have been essential to your success?

Judine: Nonfiction writing has been essential for my success. However, I think those who write fiction are recreating the characters from stories that couldn't be told by the original author. In America's past, there were triangles of relationships and stories our ancestors couldn't tell. Fiction writers often tell me they wake up in the night with characters speaking to them. I believe these are our ancestors whispering, "Write my story."

Shouldn't you be writing?

Pen to Paper
Book Resources

Learning Self-Therapy Through Writing: an experience in Creative Journaling
by Dr. Nathaniel Gadsen (Irvine, CA: Universal Publishers)

The journal explores three basic questions, who am I, what can I do, and what do I want to do? Then the book challenges you to get started today. The journal is unique because it guides you through very creative but simple exercises that help you visualize your inner most thoughts and fears, while empowering you to move forward.

Keel's Simple Diary Volume Two
by Philipp Keel (Köln, Germany: TASCHEN GmbH)

In a world where products are out as soon as they're in, where communicating without wires doesn't come without strings, and even our accessories need accessories, we need simple tools. A book that helps us look inside because we are overloaded outside.

Start Where You Are: A Journal for Self-Exploration
by Meera Lee Patel (New York, NY: TarcherPerigee)

An interactive journal designed to help readers nurture their creativity, mindfulness, and self-motivation. It helps readers navigate the confusion and chaos of daily life with a simple reminder: that by taking the time to know ourselves and what those dreams are, we can appreciate the world around us and achieve our dreams.

500 Journal Writing Prompts: Categorized Journal Prompts for Self-Discovery, Life Reflections and Creating a Compelling Future
by Mackenzie Reed (Amazon Digital Services LLC)

Anybody can feel stuck and in need of inspiration to get started or proceed with their journaling. With these 500 thought-provoking prompts you will be sure to find what you need to fill you journal with remarkable self-discovery.

*If there is a book
that you want to read,
but it hasn't been written yet,
you must be the one
to write it.*

— Toni Morrison

What Is Your Ultimate Writing Goal?

(Use words or pictures)

The United Black Writers Association, Inc.

As a cooperative non-profit organization, we bring an awareness of African American literary talent. We encourage writing and literacy for all through workshops and educational forums. Our workshop leaders and facilitators are volunteer writers/authors, who enjoy sharing their expertise.

This is our first published written work. We are open to publishing your book, beginning in 2020.

To learn more, visit **ByAnyInkNecessary.org**.

Keep In Contact

Watch other interviews online or purchase additional copies of *Writing is Essential: Use the Skills You've Got to Get the Job Done.*

Scan the QR code to watch other
By Any Ink Necessary interviews

Purchase the book on Amazon by
visiting **amzn.to/33s7UYT**

③

Mail the coupon below with your payment to:
United Black Writers Association, Inc.
c/o Judine Slaughter
PO Box 1449
Hyattsville, MD 20785

Please send me _____ paperback book(s) at the price of $17.95 each. Postage and handling is $7.00 for one book, and $3.00 for each additional book. Prices are subject to change without notice.

Name_____

Address_____

City/State/Zip Code_____

Phone_____

Email_____

CPSIA information can be obtained
at www.ICGtesting.com
Printed in the USA
BVHW031028160919
558547BV00008B/218/P

9 781733 976725